Positiv

MW01641283

How to Fight Back Against Negative Thought Patterns and Win at Life

By Michael Sloan

Copyright 2016 by Michael Sloan

Published by Make Profits Easy LLC

Profitsdaily123@aol.com

facebook.com/MakeProfitsEasy

Table of Contents

Introduction:

"Oh don't worry about it! You just need to think positively!" Have you ever heard those words and felt a frustration at that phrase? Do you sometimes feel a deep urge to smack cheerful people around? With all of the gurus, positive thinking experts and hippies out there who tell us that all we need to do is "think positive", it's surprising that so many of us are still stuck in our negative thought patterns. Or is it?

One problem with all of the people out there who say that we should just think positively is that they just tell us what we need to do. When it comes to how we can do it, we're often left without any information. Well today is that day we change that, because today we're here to talk about Thinking Positively with Action. The goal of this book is to help you learn how to think positively and how to take actions that can help cultivate a healthy mindset of positivity! We're not here with stock phrases, feel good advice and simplistic mantras. Rather we're going to dig deep and really challenge the core concepts of what leads a person to think negatively.

This book will cover three major areas that will lead to living a life of positive thinking with action. The first area is looking into the question of why we as people think negatively. The second section will talk all about how to root through the negative aspects in your own life and come to terms with the fact that change is necessary. Finally, in the third section we are going to chat about just how we can take actions that will lead to living a healthier, more positive lifestyle. It's not going to be easy, but let's face it, if it were that easy than a simple phrase would be all it takes to learn how to think positive. Let's get started.

Chapter 1: Why Are We Negative?

The first thing that we must face in our quest to learn to think positively is that most of us often think in a very negative manner. Why do we think so negatively? Well, it's a very complex answer and so it must be broken down into several large chunks.

For the most part, our negative thought patterns stem from previous experiences, things that have shaped us in such a way that cause us to think negative things. These negative experiences, especially at a young age, teach us what we believe to be truths and as such, we live out of these truths.

Consider for a moment, how we learn as children. When we look up at the sky and see a bird, we will point at it and say "bird!" Our parents say "yes, you're right!" Then we see an airplane fly by and we point again and yell out "bird!" Our parents correct us this time and say "no, that's an airplane." Up until the moment that new information is introduced to us, we will operate off of the things that we have already learned to be true. As we grow up, we start to have experiences which cause us to form a belief. Until we are corrected by an outside source, we will believe most negatives experience as true. Imagine if that child's parents had not bothered to correct him, or most likely his parents simply weren't there to correct him when he saw the airplane. He would live the rest of his life believing that airplanes are birds until someone corrects him.

The problem with negative thinking is that we often don't have anyone help us in correcting it because it's much harder to see than a simple error like mistaking a bird for a plane. Cynicism, black and white thinking, catastrophizing, polarization and other negative thought patterns are often mistook for as personality traits and we adapt to them. In some cases, such as being overly cynical, we can become proud of these negative thought patterns. They become a part of our identity and as such, we find that they become integral to who we are.

So the first thing to know about why negative thoughts are within in us is that they are bred by experiences. Either someone told us something that hurt us, something happened that caused us to believe a certain truth or we came to something on our own conclusion without anyone telling us otherwise. As these untruths and negatives took hold in our minds, they grew stronger and became more a part of our personalities. Eventually we started to recognize them as a part of ourselves and so we don't seek to change these negativities because to us they are a way of life now.

This might seem absurd to an outsider, of course. The idea that we keep negative thought processes willingly might seem like a person is willfully hurting themselves, but the truth is *they don't know any other way until corrected!* Just like the little boy who has no idea that gigantic mechanical jet isn't a bird, so do those of us who have a negative outlook on life fail to realize that we are suffering. Many times we don't even notice it because we have grown so used to the way we think.

What about you? Do you think that maybe you have some negative thought patterns that you are living out but haven't really spent lot of time thinking about them? It's normal for everyone to have some degree of negative thinking, so let's go ahead and take a look at a few major examples of what's known as a cognitive distortion. A cognitive distortion is essentially a pattern of thinking that has very specific traits. Read through the list and see if you fit any of these categories:

Black and White Thinking:

Black and white thinking, also known as polarization, is a kind of thought pattern where you judge things as either good or bad. This is taken to an extreme in a black and white thinker, however and they don't simply look at things as shades of gray, rather everything has to be good or bad. They are quick to make judgments about a situation, seeing a positive thing as good or looking at a negative thing as bad. There's no wiggle room with a black and white thinker. If a project has imperfections, it is a "failure." If they are happy with something they are "ecstatic." The extremes are intense with a polarized thinker and they often live out of these extremes. Tension can rise when they begin sorting people into the good or bad category and oftentimes they will find themselves dealing with themselves and others harshly.

Catastrophizing:

Catastrophizing is the act of thinking about something and taking it to the most dangerous and illogical conclusion. For example, if someone is on an airplane and they hear a bumping sound, if they were a catastrophizer they would quickly come to think that the plane was going to crash, going immediately to the worst case scenario as opposed to trying to figure out what made that noise. In relationships a catastrophizer might become obsessive, worried when their friends don't text them back that their friend is either dead or now hates them. Someone who has a catastrophic thought pattern often finds themselves constantly in a state of worry or anxiety.

Emotional Reasoning:

Emotional reasoning is where a person tends to allow their feeling to influence what they believe to be true instead of looking at the reality of the situation. For example, if a person feels that they are ugly, they will believe they are ugly, regardless of what others around them tell them. An emotional truth creates the specific reality for said individual and they live in a constant state of intense, emotional pain because of this false reality.

Filtering:

There are usually positives and negatives to most situations. Life is rarely one dimension and as such, there are good things and bad things in just about any situation. A person who has a filtering type of thought pattern will zero in on the bad, focusing primarily on the things that are negative in the situation as opposed to looking at the big picture and seeing the truth for what it is. Filtering often makes a bad situation worse and negates the chance for any kind of good thing to be seen in positive situations.

Personalization:

Personalization is where an individual sees themselves as primarily to blame for everything that happens around them, regardless of whether they had a direct hand in it or not. If someone with that personalization thought pattern were to see a car accident that was nearby them, they might think that they were somehow responsible for it. If some kind of tragedy befell a friend, they might feel they have something to with the situation, even if they did not.

Over-generalization:

When a person over-generalizes, they are reacting to a very small specific amount of information and then they apply it to an entire situation. For example, if it rains once on the way to a picnic, the over-generalizer will say "it always rains on a picnic." They think in always and never statements. In their relationships they might say "you always talk about yourself' or "you never pay attention to me." In their minds they might feel that the situation always happens one way or another due to previous experiences. This can lead them to believing something different from reality and reacting differently than other people would. How would you react as if every single time you went on a picnic, it rained? Regardless of the reality, the over-generalizer reacts that way each time, even if it only happened once.

Mind Reading:

Someone who has the negative thought patterns of mind reading might find themselves trying to guess what other people are thinking. This mind reading often believes that others are thinking negatively or that their intentions are meant to cause them harm. Mind reading is a way for a person to jump to conclusions, inferring what they believe about someone without having sufficient evidence. Thinking “no one has texted me all week, they must hate me,” is an example of mind reading. The only piece of information this individual has is that they haven’t been texted and with that information they are able to jump to the conclusion that they are disliked.

Giving Up Control:

Some individuals believe that they honestly do not have any control in their life. Things are always someone else's fault. They struggle to take responsibility because they honestly believe that other factors are always responsible for their behavior. "I'm sorry I was angry with you but I was hungry" is a statement that gives up control for an active choice. Instead they are choosing to blame some other source for what happened. This can also apply to accusing people of making us feel certain emotions. When a person transfers responsibility to someone or something else, they are adopting a thought pattern of refusing to change themselves.

Splitting:

Splitting is the attitude of all or nothing. Either a person is willing to keep their room absolutely spotless or it will be an absolute cesspool of filth. Either they are going to work out every single day or they will not work out at all. This all or nothing attitude infiltrates just about every facet of an individual's life. It can cause immense strain on their relationships, friendships and choices in life. The idea that things have to be perfect or they are terrible will essentially create a false belief that things are either much better or much worse than they really are.

When we look at all of these negative thought patterns, it's no wonder that the world is in such a state! The seeds of these various different patterns work to sabotage us as we begin to try and adapt to new patterns. The brain is very interested in confirming what it knows to be true. Once we adopt a negative thought pattern, our minds become very protective of these thought patterns and as such they grow to become a part of us.

So why do we develop such patterns of thought? Do negative experiences really have the ability to affect how we look at life? The answer is a resounding yes! All of the negative things that you experience in your life, especially at the early stages, have a lot to do with how we begin to develop these negative patterns of thought. Let's move onto the next chapter to take a look at why our brains develop these kinds of thought processes.

Chapter 2: Shame is The Name

Let's talk about what leads our minds to begin to develop the unhealthy patterns of negative thinking. When we are young, our cognitive structures are relatively new and as we develop, we experience a lot of information that tell us things. We are greedy to devour all of the new information possible. When we learn a new word, it's exciting. When we discover a new concept we're happy to take it as a fact. But what happens when we experience something negative towards ourselves? What do we do when we begin to experience a fact that tells us something bad about ourselves? That is where shame begins.

Imagine for a moment a little girl trying to get her father's attention. He is busy working at his computer and doesn't have time to look over at her. She's four years old and is adamant to have his attention but he simply won't look over at her. She wants his attention, his delight and him to be proud of her, but in that moment, she receives none of the things that she's looking for. Her mind is faced with a situation and it begins to interpret the events in such a way that it creates shame. Rather than simply say "Daddy isn't interested in me right now," the four-year-old brain says "I'm not interesting to Daddy." This creates a seed of doubt, a feeling that eventually leads to shame.

Shame is a powerful motivator and many of us experience it at an early, developmental stage in our lives. These feelings of shame are so powerful that the mind itself seeks for ways to protect from it. This often develops patterns of thinking that are designed to prevent from feeling shame or to block unpleasant emotions entirely. At a young age, this process of trying to learn how to avoid shame leads a person to develop specific personality traits that are defensive in nature. After the brain develops a position, it then begins to look for all things that agree with that position. This is a validating behavior, something that explains why a person feels the way they do.

For example, if this young girl grows up to 10 and finds that people at school are not interested in playing with her at recess. Her mind will immediately use that as a validating position for why she is uninteresting. The brain will take this information and use it as fuel in the bid to convince this girl that she isn't interesting. This is a shameful experience and the shame of being someone not worthy of attention can manifest itself in many different ways. She could grow wild and out of control in a desperate bid to get attention. She could become withdrawn and afraid of the world, desperate to avoid feeling the pain of rejection or she could become high functioning and industrious to show everyone that she is interesting. Regardless of how she acts, the internal feelings are driven by shame.

Our negative thought patterns tend to stem from experiences that shape the way we view the world. We then begin to develop behavior that validates why we feel the way we do. As such, our negative thinking patterns grow and grow until we become primarily dominated by them. The shame that we endure at such an early age simply goes on to contribute to a lot of different factors, such as increased negative thinking, unhealthy thought patterns and loss of self-esteem. Let's take a look at some of the symptoms of shame on our thought processes as a whole:

Poor Self Image:

Shame essentially tells us that we are bad. The difference between shame and guilt is that guilt tells us that we did something wrong. It says "hey, you've broken a law or hurt someone else." Guilt leads to the ability to confess or repent for our wrongdoing and that allows for us to change. Guilt is productive, it has a purpose. It's useful and healthy for us to feel guilty when we've done a bad thing, but what does shame tell us?

Shame doesn't say that we did something bad, rather it tells us that we are bad. These feelings of shame start at an early age, usually when we are shamed for an action or behavior. At some point we begin to take them as truth and in the process of believing that we ourselves are bad, we begin to develop a poor sense of self.

Low self-esteem isn't simply just thinking poorly about yourself. It is not easily remedied by thinking positively either. Low self-esteem creates an environment in which a person always feels as if they are not good enough. The results of having a poor sense of self-worth can be staggering. They can develop a series of cognition distortions relating to the self and can generally cause a person's mind to become clouded by the idea that they will always be this way. In other words, shame creates negative thinking because it tells a person that they themselves aren't valuable. How can someone who believes they are worthless think positively?

Negative Self-Talk

Working with shame hand in hand is negative self-talk. Everyone talks to themselves, in their heads or out loud, it's just part of who we are as human beings. Negative self-talk is where the words and thoughts you communicate to yourself, about yourself are overwhelmingly unkind. This can also be called the Inner Critic, that voice within you that criticizes your every action and decision.

The Inner Critic can plague the best of us and even those who work extremely hard to become successful in life might find that their inner voice is relentless in its assault of their inner self. Negative self-talk is a reflection of how we feel about our shame, it's an active way in which we give into the idea that we are worthless or without value. Remember, shame talks in "I am" statements, and you will find that if you struggle with a fierce inner critic, it will usually talk in such a way too.

Unhealthy Fears:

Fear can be a perfectly healthy thing to have. Fear often protects us from making poor decisions or putting ourselves in harm's way. Fear indicates that going into that dark alley late at night might not be the best idea or that perhaps we should get dressed fully before going to the ballet recital. There is a healthy and appropriate place for fear in our lives, but what's not appropriate is the development of shame based fears.

Shame based fears are feelings such as fear of rejection or fear of failure. The shame based fear stems from the idea that if we experience negativity, we will experience a greater sense of shame. For example, if a wife is afraid of failure, she might be greatly afraid of trying out a new dinner recipe for her husband, for fear of feeling shame if it went wrong. And if it does go wrong, she will experience an even greater amount of fear and distress, fearing the absolute worst, which in this case is being ashamed for having done poorly on a meal.

Of course, who hasn't made a poor choice when cooking a meal? A failed meal is nothing more than a fact of life and it happens from time to time. When shame based fear exists, it can make such a concept as failing at a new recipe feel like it is life or death.

Guilt:

Shame also creates guilt. This guilt is different from the normal, healthy guilt because this guilt is unsolvable. When someone is feeling guilty for something they have done wrong, the natural solution isn't to try and not feel guilty anymore, the solution is to atone for the wrong they have done. But when there was no wrong because the guilt is self-inflicted, it can lead to a great amount of distress and frustration in the life of the one carrying that guilt.

Shame creates these feelings of guilt because oftentimes a person dealing with intense patterns of shame feel that they are somehow to blame for their emotions, feelings or decisions. They take upon a colossal burden and grow heavy with the weight of the world. The worst part is that they aren't able to solve their guilt since it's self-inflicted.

Anxiety:

Shame can also create anxious thought patterns in an individual. They grow worried about how they are perceived by others and find themselves obsessing over the smallest things. Anxiety unchecked can develop into full blown neurosis or obsession. This can leave a person dealing with repeated, obsessive thoughts about a problem or might leave them paralyzed to even deal with social problems.

As you can see, the effects of shame are intense and widespread. Remember, if our goal is to learn how to think positive with action, we're going to have to identify the factors within us that cause us to think negatively. It's not good enough to think that we can pave over bad behaviors with good ones. Rather we must get to a place of being able to recognize what drives our actions inside of our heads and learn how to heal from them.

Hopefully at this point you'll have been able to recognize a few negative thought patterns in yourself. Whether it's expecting things to always go wrong, catastrophizing or experiencing intense anxiety, these negative thoughts will threaten our ability to learn to live healthy, positive lives. Thinking positive is only one half of the equation, learning to sift through our own negative experiences and recognize them is the other half. Let's move onto the next chapter.

Chapter 3: Paving the Road to Change

Change isn't easy. Over the course of our lives we have worked very hard to develop patterns of thought that often work against our best interests. Why? Because the brain is naturally defensive of the truths that it accepts early on. Once you've learned something and believed it to be true, your brain will fight to keep that information as valid as possible.

Imagine how long of a distance it is from the first time you began having negative world views and outlooks on life to right now. Chances are it's more than just a few years' time. These things start out at such a young age and they take root. They firmly connect themselves to our identity to the point where we stop noticing it at all.

These behaviors become what's known as an automatic behavior. An automatic behavior is essentially a decision or choice you make immediately without taking any notice of it. Apologies in advance, but think about your breathing for a moment. Do you feel a little weird now? Chances are, you were breathing entirely automatically until it was pointed out, at that point your mind takes over on the function. Our automatic behaviors often happen without our permission and as such, we find that we are reacting more than we are acting.

No one wants to have cognitive distortions. No one wants to have shame or obsessive thoughts in their lives. But the fact is, until we become aware of their existence within us, we won't be able to address them properly. There's an old joke about a man who goes to see the doctor and says "doctor, no matter where I touch on my body, it hurts. I touch my nose, I feel immense pain, if I touch my feet, still pain. No matter where I touch, there's always pain. What's wrong with me?" The doctor replies "I believe your finger is broken, sir." When we aren't aware of the thing that is the root cause of our behavior, we can make the mistake of thinking the symptoms are the problem. Just like the man who thinks the pain all over his body is the problem, so can we make the mistake of believing that our nervousness, cynicism or polarization is the result of outside sources.

The truth is, we are responsible entirely for what is happening within our own minds and hearts. We have the power to investigate these negative patterns, find out where they come from and correct them. This process of self-discovery can be somewhat intense though and might bring up feelings that are rather unpleasant. Feelings are just indicators of what we are experiencing however and despite how unpleasant they feel they aren't going to harm you. What is going to harm you, in the long run, is ignoring the process of introspection due to any unpleasantness.

So what is the first step in the road to changing our negative thinking? It's the step of learning to stop and look within. It's known as introspection. Here's a step by step process in how to stop and gauge your own internal.

Introspection Step One: Slow Down

Introspection is the art of being able to stop, take a breath and look at your own thought processes. It requires a certain amount of self-awareness and self-awareness takes time to cultivate. If you're busy running around trying to get stuff done, work, take care of the kids and catch the big game, you won't really have the time to look within.

Introspection requires stillness and calmness, it's the act of being able to reflect upon what you are thinking and take stock of what you feel. The first step to being introspective is slowing down and making sure that you have quiet time to reflect and relax. You won't be able to change your thought patterns overnight, but you will be able to cultivate a mindset of looking inward if you make a point to rest and relax.

Tips for slowing down include:

- Take a few minutes out of your day to rest in silence.
- Find somewhere quiet and serene to be able to reflect.
- Learn meditation or take up prayer as a way to learn to quiet yourself.
- Make a regular point of spending at least fifteen minutes reflecting before you go to sleep each night.

Introspection Step 2: Reflect

Once you've slowed down and have spent time learning how to sit in silence and relax yourself, it's time to start putting energy into learning how to reflect on your own thoughts. Watching your own thoughts can be hard, because they are often automatic. They happen immediately and once you begin to start questioning the very things you are thinking you might begin to find out that some of those thoughts are quite negative.

Reflection is necessary to understand just what you are thinking day to day. Oftentimes we have emotional reactions to things immediately. We feel anger, frustration, sorrow or hopelessness the moment something negative comes our way and we feel powerless to change it. It is only when we begin to reflect on what led to these reactions can we hope to change them.

The art of reflection is looking back on your day and thinking about the choices you've made. Think about the thoughts that you've had and really scrutinize your actions. If we're looking for negative thought patterns, start asking yourself questions. Questions like "did I really feel this way," or "am I really sure it happened that way?"

Here are some ways to reflect on the things and events that have happened in your day:

Keeping a journal can be an excellent tool to begin the process of consciously reflecting each and every day of your life. By making a habit of keeping a journal, not only do you get the benefit of seeing your life change and grow day to day, it gives you insight into your own thought processes. A journal can be used to reflect in the moment and also gives you a tool to look at your own thoughts over time to look for patterns. If there are negative thought patterns in your thinking, it will become visible once you start reading through your own thoughts.

- Learn to stop and identify what you are feeling in the moment rather than just giving in to your emotions. For example, if you begin to feel angry, anxious, nervous, irate or sad, don't just go with the emotions. It's important to stop and actually ask yourself why are you feeling that way. Look for the root of the emotion and over time you will discover where these negative emotions are coming from. Of course, it's not easy to stop in the moment when you are first beginning, so make a habit of reflecting afterwards first. Any time you have a moment of intense negativity, try to look back at it during your time of reflection and ask yourself why you reacted the way you did. Over time, you will eventually be able to reach a point where you can catch yourself becoming emotional or negative during the event, but at the beginning it's best to just learn how to look back first.

- If you're really brave, ask a friend whom you trust about your behaviors. Make sure it's someone that you're really comfortable talking to, maybe a mentor, a religious authority or a counselor. They might be able to point out things that might be harder for you to see. Remember, the human mind is pretty biased towards itself and can often be blind to its own failings. Having someone that you trust tell you of areas where you can improve can often lead to great growth in your life, if you are willing to accept the feedback. The danger of asking others when you aren't ready is that you might become defensive. Ask only when you are ready to hear what hurts.

- Pain is to be expected when reflecting on our own nature. The human ego is fragile and often seeks to protect itself. Having to face a reality where our behavior is less than stellar can often cause us to feel vulnerable, exposed or embarrassed. The whole point in learning about these problems isn't so that we can just beat ourselves up over our actions, it's to inspire change. There isn't much hope for us if we are looking to avoid pain because oftentimes these negative thought patterns emerge because of our desire to protect ourselves. Abandoning the desire to protect the self will enable for you to grow far past your comfort zone and in the process, you will begin to experience a positive life change!

Introspection Step 3: Identify

After you've spent sufficient time looking at yourself, trying to gauge where you are at in your thought patterns, it's time for you to identify where your negativity is. Ideas don't do well when they stay in the head as abstracts. You must learn to take them out from your head and put them down on paper. Once you see what's in front of you, the idea becomes concrete and you can defeat whatever is in front of you.

Have you learned that you might be somewhat of a narcissist? Put it down! Do you realize that every time you have a problem you react as if it were the end of the world? That's worth writing down. Whatever you start to realize about yourself, place it down on paper, not to judge yourself but to show you what you have been living as. The struggle in learning to identify your own negative qualities is that shame will often show up and use those qualities as reasons for why you are worthless. "See?" shame will say, pointing at your realization that you're someone who is always right, "you are worthless!"

Recognizing something for what it is isn't evidence that you are a bad person. If anything it's just recognizing that you are human. Perfectionism is just another tool that shame utilizes to keep you from changing your life. Shame demands that you be perfect and since you can never achieve that, you'll always feel beaten and held down. Don't let the realization that you have imperfections in yourself stop you from seeking change!

Identification is the last and final step to introspection. The whole point of looking within yourself is being able to identify the things that are within you that contribute to living a life of negative thinking. We can't learn to think positively until we learn the negative things that lie within us, as those negative thoughts will actively supplant any attempts to live a positive life. The best way to think positive with action is to first identity the negative thoughts going on inside your head. What do we do after that? Well, we have to take an assessment!

An assessment is looking further at your negative thinking behaviors and figuring out how harsh they are. Don't make the mistake of thinking in a simple good or bad scale, that's black and white thinking. Instead we need to be able to assess just how severe our negative thoughts are. Let's take a look at a step by step method to assess any type of negative thinking.

Assessment Step 1: Determine How It Impacts Your Life

If you were to score your negative thought pattern, whichever ones they are, how would they rate on a scale of 1-10 in interfering with your life? Someone who catastrophizes so much to the point where they can't leave the house would rank a 10 on the scale, whereas someone who occasionally worries about end of the world phenomena might rank on a 3.

The purpose of establishing a scale of impact is for you to be able to see just how deeply you are affected by each thought process. I believe that we all experience many different kinds of negative thought patterns from time to time. A mother might sometimes grow worried when her children don't come home five minutes after dark and a man might find himself kicking himself for a poor business decision. So don't think just because you feel certain negative thought patterns that it's a way of life for you.

We all have them on occasion, so we're really just looking for the thought patterns that are either consistent, severe or cause negative results in real life. In order to determine the impact, consider these following questions.

- Does your thought pattern cause you consistent trouble?
- Do you find your quality of life diminished due to these thoughts?
- Do you struggle to get through the day because of these thoughts?
- Have these thoughts ever caused severe reactions within you?

After you've answered those questions for each of your negative thought patterns, you should be able to discern a score from that. We don't have a scoring guide because each person is different and numbering the severity is really just a way for you to have your own internal understanding of how much it affects you. Low scores don't necessarily mean that these thought patterns should be ignored and high scores don't indicate that you're in serious trouble either. The point is just for you to understand where you are, so that as you focus on getting through the healing process and you can give more attention to each area.

Assessment Step 2: Ask Where They Come From

Once you have a solid understanding of what your negative thought patterns are and how they affect your life, it's now time for you to spend some time figuring out where you get them from. We acquire negative thought patterns from outside sources, they don't just spring up on their own. (**Please note: we are discussing ways of thinking, not mental health disorders. Some negative thought patterns might spring from physical**

issues with the brain and should only be diagnosed from a licensed mental health professional. If you suspect that your struggles are caused by brain chemistry or you have history of mental illness in your family, please see a mental health professional. Don't be embarrassed and don't be afraid to talk to your doctor about depression or other mental health problems. Just as we shouldn't be embarrassed about having the flu, we shouldn't have to feel singled out by the fact that we are struggling with mental health as well. You aren't alone!)

Negative thought patterns are learned behaviors. We experience them either through inference or through being explicitly taught. Let's discuss each one separately.

Inference:

Inference isn't explicitly stated, rather it's something that we pick up as we go. For example, if a child sees that his parents are always worried about finances and that whenever an unexpected bill arrives they become extremely panicked, he learns through inference that unexpected things equal disaster. As he grows up, he might develop the trait of being worried when money problems occur. It might even translate to a general thought pattern of being extremely tight with his money and always checking his bank account.

Our primary mode of learning is through inference. This can be seen in language. For example, when a child hears a new word, they might look at the context of the situation and learn the word. This happens when someone is learning language from immersion as well. If you are in the company of German speakers, you might pick up a word when someone points to a piece of bread and says "Sie passierien das Brot." Question: what did you think that phrase meant? Most likely you inferred that the sentence meant "pass the bread", in which case you would be correct. You looked at the situation and inferred what the words mean.

As we grow and experience the world around us, we pick up a lot through inference. Most of our negative thought patterns will often come from inference. A parent who scolds a child angrily when they get a low report card will begin to infer that good grades equal self-worth. Oftentimes what we infer can be wrong, but since we are not being explicitly taught these lessons, we have no way of signaling that we are learning such things.

This means that as we grow in our lives, we can pick up very unhealthy ways of thinking and relating without anyone noticing. Our parents, no matter how hard they try, can't really pick up on inference. It's only when a child's behavior begins to manifest in negativity that it can be addressed and oftentimes the symptoms are addressed and not the root cause.

As you begin to sift through your own emotional beliefs and reactions, you might benefit from taking a hard look at some of the behaviors you have learned from your upbringing. You might be able to trace specific thought patterns to inference from actions that your educators took. Some inference might have been extremely negative, such as parental abandonment or scolding when you had good intentions. Other inferences might have seemed harmless or were unintentional but ended up teaching you more by actions. We are imitative creatures and we learn to imitate what others say and do. We also imitate what is unsaid and in our formative years. We might cling onto that which is taught but not spoken.

The purpose of learning where your thought patterns come from isn't to blame your parents, teachers or other important figures in your life. There's no value in angrily pointing back at the past and it doesn't do any good to wish things had been different. If you want to learn where you are going, you have to learn where you have been. Negative patterns are unconscious and automatic, in order to bring them to the surface we need to be able to see where they come from. Once you know what has caused these patterns, you can then begin to go through the healing process. But if they stay in the back of your mind, forever unexamined, you won't really be able to fix anything.

Ask yourself these questions as you begin to look for learning through inference:

- Did my parents act this way?
- How did I come to this conclusion?
- Is my thinking rational or irrational about this subject?
- Do I remember when my change in behavior began?
- Did anyone try to correct me on my behavior or did it go unnoticed?

Taught Behaviors:

Unfortunately, sometimes we learn negative thought patterns because we were directly taught lessons that transferred negative thinking patterns to us. This is oftentimes a case of neglect or even outright parental abuse. A child who is told by his father that he is worthless will come to believe it, or a daughter whose mother teaches her to obsess over her looks and weight will often develop significant anxieties.

When someone is put into an unfortunate position of receiving negative information about themselves, especially when they are a child, they soak up these negative patterns of thinking and begin to exhibit such behaviors as transferred to them. In other words, when we are in a vulnerable place and there are untrustworthy people in our lives, we might be damaged by what they tell us.

This damage can be extremely intense and might take more than just a single book to overcome. The wounds that we bear as we grow up can significantly hamper our ability to live quality lives and even as we work to overcome our negative thought patterns, we might find that these wounds drag us down. It's important to know that when we are told wrong things about ourselves that it doesn't have to be true. Just because someone tells you that you are worthless, dumb or insignificant, either directly or indirectly, that doesn't mean you have to live that way. Our brains will take whatever beliefs have been thrown our way and begin to adopt these patterns as truth.

But just because we have thought that these things are true in the past doesn't' mean we have to accept them in the future. The purpose behind learning to assess your negative thought patterns is to ultimately be free of them. Whether you were taught to think this way or if someone told you that you have no value, you are not required to live under that belief. You can be free to heal from this damage. It just takes determination, willpower and a little bit of courage. Are you ready?

Chapter 4: Healing from Negative Thought Patterns

The process in learning to heal from a negative pattern of thought is difficult but worth it. Remember, as we've discussed before, it's not about just replacing a bad behavior with a good behavior. It's about learning what the healing process is and then moving in a positive direction. You don't get out of a hole by covering the hole, you get out of the hole by climbing your way up.

So how do we climb our way out of these holes that our negative thought patterns have dug for us? Well there's several different steps and methods you can apply. Let's go through each method one at a time. If you find something that you think will suit you well, take it and use it as your own. If you don't agree with a certain method or you find one to be something you don't like, don't think you have to adopt it. The best path to healing is one that you will follow to the end. If you don't buy into the path that is being presented, chances are you won't finish it.

Healing Step One: Take Responsibility

It's not easy to take responsibility for our lives, but it is a necessary component. You must be able to look in the mirror and say to yourself "I am responsible for the way I act and think." This might be painful at first, but don't focus on what causes you pain. Shame might try to make you shrink away from taking responsibility, telling you that if you own up to where you are in life that you will somehow die. But the truth is that you must be responsible if you want to heal.

Your job is to take care of yourself. No one else has to live with you at the end of the day, no one else has to deal with your own thoughts and inner psyche. This means that you and you alone are the only human responsible for your own actions. Automatic thoughts and unconscious decisions are automatic because you allow them to be. Negative thought patterns exist within you because you have chosen to let them be there.

Don't mistake what I am saying here. I am not saying that you are bad, stupid or wrong for having these negative thoughts. Chances are you didn't really have a choice when they were put on you long ago, but the fact that you are choosing to carry them still is a conscious decision. Once you have realized that you have a certain way of thinking, you are responsible for what you do with it. This can be intimidating but it's also the only way to heal from where you have been.

When you take responsibility for your actions, your decisions and your choices, you are free to climb out of the hole. The only person keeping you down there is you! It's not easy and it can be painful having to face the fact that you are there willingly, but don't let shame hold you back. Shame's desire is to always keep you down, to tell you that you are worthless and to put you in a cage. Your desire, by coming to this book and spending this time on personal development, is to be free of negative thoughts and you can only achieve that by allowing yourself to heal.

So starting now, starting today you are to look at yourself and say "I am responsible for my thoughts, feelings and behaviors. I might not always make the best choices and I might not always understand why I do the things that I do, but I can and will change for the better. Today I am making the choice to own up to my choices and to live fully each day."

Healing Step Two: Remove the Victim Mentality

Many times as we develop our negative feelings and thought patterns we begin to believe that we are helpless in the situation. Sometimes we discover that becoming a victim will protect us from more negative experiences or in some situations even give us positive experiences such as sympathy or assistance from others. The desire to be a victim can be very strong when we are thinking negative thoughts. Our minds darken and we only focus on the pain and problems that we are struggling with, we become self-obsessed in a way and begin only thinking of how things go wrong for us.

The victim mentality often coincides with negative thinking. For some reason, we adopt a position of helplessness that both removes our agency and our ability to act. If we are a victim, then we are not responsible because honestly, we're just trying our best. The truth is, being a victim is entirely a state of mind.

Even if you were harmed in the past, even if you still suffer from other people's actions, you must know that you aren't meant to live your life as a victim. You cannot be victorious if you live as if the wounds that you bear are still affecting you. You must learn from the things that have hurt you and move forward. The mind of the victim is stuck in the past, obsessing over pain and fearing the future, but the mind of the victor welcomes the future with excitement and vigor. You are not a victim and you never have to be one. You always have a choice and even if you experience pain from others, you can still conquer that pain by allowing it to shape you for the better and not for the worst!

Healing Step Three: Challenge Your Assumptions and Beliefs

Whenever you make an assumption, stop to challenge it. What does the word loser actually mean when your inner critic calls you one? What does it mean to actually feel worthless? Is the worst thing always guaranteed to happen?

When you make a habit of regularly challenging what you believe and assume, you will discover that many times our beliefs tend to be automatic. Why do you think that you are bad at something? Why do you believe that your husband secretly hates you? When you start to question what you believe, you might end up hitting walls faster than you realize. A negative belief exists for some reason, but oftentimes we don't stop to question why we think a specific way. We often look for supporting statements to validate what we believe, but we don't usually look past the validating statements. Rather than think to ourselves "my best friend said something sarcastic, that proves he hates me," we must think "why do I believe that my friend hates me? What evidences support that objectively?"

Making a habit of stopping whenever you begin to feel your negative thought patterns arise will build a discipline of stopping to evaluate what your beliefs are. Oftentimes our negative thoughts are based on faulty beliefs that will continue to bother us until they are challenged. Examining evidence, asking where you think those thoughts come from and trying to ascertain just what the core belief that is affecting you at that moment will lead you to not simply being able to challenge it, but to eliminate that belief as well.

Beliefs change over time and only after sufficient repetition. The brain uses neural pathways to essentially carve in your brain certain ideas. The more an idea is repeated, the more hard wired your brain is. Think of it kind of like a trail in a forest. The more a trail is stepped on, the less grass will grow on that trail. When there is significant foot traffic, that trail will essentially become permanent. On the other hand, if a trail is neglected for a specific amount of time, it will naturally begin to become overgrown by foliage and grass and will eventually be forgotten.

Your beliefs, especially the negative ones, are well embedded pieces of memories that will not easily be eliminated. But each time you opt to guide your thinking away from the negative belief trail and towards a positive belief trail, it will weaken the trail as a whole. Eventually that trail will cease to exist because you are no longer using it.

The more you give in to a negative belief, the more you will behave as if it were real. The inverse is also true, the more you give in to a positive belief, the more real it will become. This takes us to step four.

Healing Step Four: Develop Positive Beliefs

Don't think of a white elephant. How did you do? Chances are you thought of a white elephant, despite the fact that you were told not to think about it. This is because the brain must fill a space. It cannot simply disregard a fact or idea. So as we begin to work our way out of negative thought patterns, we must begin to develop new, positive beliefs. This is where positive thinking finally comes in. Remember, the goal is not just to try and think positively. The goal is to remove the negative thoughts and replace them with positive ones. And positive thoughts start with positive beliefs.

As we've talked about earlier, when you are forced to confront a negative belief, you are putting yourself in the captain's chair, choosing to go down a different path. You can give into your negative belief and continue reinforcing what you think or you can take another option. That other option can't be nothing. You can't think "oh don't think negatively" and expect for it to work. Like the elephant example earlier, your brain must fill the space with something.

This is where positive beliefs come in. When we remove one negative belief, we must replace it with a positive one. This involves making a conscious effort to challenge the negative thought patterns with positive ones. For example, if someone is dealing with the fact that their thinking often goes to the worst possible situation regardless of what it is, they are going to have to replace that type of belief (Everything is going to fall apart) with a new belief

(Sometimes things don't work out and that's okay)

This process isn't necessarily the easiest, especially when we have a good amount of negative beliefs that have built up over time in our heads. These beliefs, when unchecked, will continue to wreak havoc on our lives and break our hearts and minds.

So how do we develop positive beliefs? Is it really as simple as just thinking something else? Well, it's a complicated process so let's break it down step by step.

Positive Belief Development Step One: Accept Imperfection

If you want to learn to think positive, you're going to have to have realize that imperfection is a part of life. We are not perfect beings and as such, our ability to live perfect lives is also impossible. If you demand the impossible from yourself, you will never get it.

Many times our negative thought patterns are demanding that we live perfect lives. So one of the healthiest ways of thinking is to accept your imperfection and take that as a fact. Develop the belief that it's okay to fail, to be wrong, to be laughed at. The worst case scenario in your life isn't that you are wrong or that people find out that you aren't perfect. The worst case is when your desire for perfection leads you to a life of fear and pain.

Positive Belief Development Step Two: Counter Self-Talk

Your self-talk will most likely echo and reflect what your beliefs are. They will tell you that you are dumb, idiotic, unlovable or other unkind things. If you're looking to develop a positive outlook on life, you've got to be quick to challenge and counter any negative self-talk that you encounter. When your inner critic begins to voice its disgust with you, you must be able to reply with good things. Then meditate on the things that are true in your life. When the self-critic begins to tell you that you don't have value, counter with the fact that you do have value. The idea that you are worthless has no foundation and the fact that other people care about you proves otherwise.

Combat the self-talk quickly and actively. Don't allow for it to tell you things that aren't true. If you find this to be too difficult, try ignoring the critic instead. Who says you have to listen to what it says? If someone in real life is saying mean things to you, do you have to believe them? Just because that voice comes from inside doesn't mean you have to take the words as truth. You can be free from negative self-talk just realizing that it isn't true and that you don't have to listen to that channel anymore. Turn off those tapes and don't let them repeat!

Positive Belief Development Step Three: Develop Self-Acceptance

If you are at peace with yourself, then you never have to worry about what other people think. One of the most core beliefs that you should develop is that you are perfectly okay just the way you are. Other people might try and change you. They will tell you that you need to do this, that and the other thing in order to meet their approval. But, if you stopped and realized that you are just fine how you are, you will be able to move past these negative things that hold you back.

Developing a love for yourself can help silence that inner critic as well as begin a powerful healing process that leads you out of living under the shadow of shame. Shame says I am bad, whereas self-love says I am good. You don't fight a negative with another negative, you can't say to shame "you are bad, so stop making me feel bad," rather we say to shame "I don't know what you're talking about, I'm perfectly fine the way I am. I am good."

One powerful belief that is often pounded into our heads at an early stage in our life is that loving yourself is selfish. They want you to be self-sacrificing and hating towards yourself, as if that somehow makes a person kinder and generous. Someone who is at peace with who they are and loves themselves won't feel the urge to show how strong they are or how important they are. Instead, they choose to live quiet lives of dignity and share their kindness with others. Since they don't need to demand that others love them because they themselves are filled with love, they are free from catastrophic thinking, obsessive anxieties and ungrounded fears. They can reach across the aisle and help out others, acting from a place of peace and tranquility.

There is nothing wrong with loving yourself, there is nothing wrong with being happy with the way you were made. We were made to feel love and there's nothing wrong with that. Selfishness isn't about how you feel, its' about how you act. There's no merit to being a crass, selfish individual but oftentimes that selfishness stems from a lack of feeling loved. If a person were to be fulfilled in themselves, they wouldn't need to rely on greed to fulfill them.

So how can we develop a greater love for ourselves? Try:

- Learning to be alone and be happy.
- Take delight in the abilities and skills that you have.
- Take good care of yourself, be disciplined. It's not loving to give a child everything it demands, neither it is very loving for you to give into your bodies constant demand to laze around the house and eat junk food.

- Forgive yourself for the actions that you have done wrong. Just as you would forgive a friend for hurting you, so you must learn to say “I forgive you” to the mirror.

Healing Step Five: Practice Daily

Healing is not a one-time affair. We do not suddenly go from being a negative thinking individual to a positive one overnight. It takes time and effort. It will take a daily practice of focusing on changing a little bit each and every day. If you aren’t ready to set aside the time to develop good habits or if you aren’t willing to challenge each negative thought that comes your way, you will not reach a place of healing.

Consistency is necessary if you want to grow and change past your natural negative thought patterns. You must make it a point to treat each day as a new one and work toward winning the best possible victories as you work to integrate healthy, positive beliefs. The negative thought patterns that you have developed will often be deep and strong. They will not vanish in an hour. But with steady, repeated focus of learning to think positively, focusing on reflecting and becoming aware of our own thoughts, we will eventually leave the negative thoughts behind and go on to live out healthy, uplifting thoughts.

Healing Step Six: See a Professional

You don't have to go on a healing journey alone. If you find it beneficial, it might not be a bad idea to reach out and look for some professional assistance. A counselor or spiritual advisor can assist you in learning to move past your negative thoughts and help you learn to talk out your feelings or frustrations. A good counselor would be able to share what they see and hear as you talk. If you aren't comfortable with the healing process, having an additional person to walk you through it would be extremely useful.

There might be a temptation to feel embarrassed about wanting help from a professional, or you might falsely believe that professional assistance is only for those who are "messed up." But the truth is that there are millions of perfectly adjusted people who go to see counselors for assistance in their own healing journey. The idea that there is somehow something inherently shameful about admitting there is pain and struggle is just another false belief that is trying to keep you where you are. The brain, at its core, wants to stay the same and healers of the mind often will help move past such negative thoughts. Don't give into the false idea that seeing professional assistance is an admission of failure. Instead see it as a victory because you are choosing to put your old thoughts away and look for a new and exciting way of living life.

Chapter 5: Actions to Think Positively

Now that we've worked so hard to get our negative thoughts under control and have started building up positive beliefs, it's time to start taking actions that will help contribute to our positivity. This is part of the package of learning how to think positively through action. Certain actions that you take can affect how you think on a daily basis and we're going to take a look at several different ways you can learn to think positively.

Positive Action One: Develop Gratitude

Gratitude is one of the most powerful emotional experiences in the world. When someone is grateful, it's because they are looking on the bright side of life. Developing a spirit of gratitude lets you see the good things, regardless of where you are. Learning to be content and grateful are one in the same.

Gratitude isn't pretending that bad things aren't bad, rather it is looking for reasons to be happy with where you are in life. It's about making a list of the things that are going well and sticking to that list when times get tough. The more grateful you become, the more satisfied you will be with your life. In fact, gratitude is considered to be one of the most desirable traits when it comes to having a high quality of life, because the more grateful you are, the happier you will be.

So how can we develop gratitude? We can:

- Write out a list of all the things we are thankful for
- Slow down and take notice of the things that we often take for granted

- Reflect on our relationships and realize how dependent we have been on the kindness of others
- Spend time in meditation thinking about all of the things that you are happy with
- Learn to enjoy the small things and be thankful for everything, even rain on a picnic.
- Express it constantly
- When you feel the urge to complain, give thanks instead

Positive Action Two: Look for the Positives

Two men are behind prison bars, they look outside, one sees mud but the other sees stars. This little rhyme shows how where we look can reinforce what we feel about the world. By making a habit of always looking for the positive things in your life, you can avoid many of the headaches and stressors that exist by focusing too much on the negative. Look for the stars regardless of what situation you are in.

We can learn to look for the positives by:

- Making a point to name at least one good thing in a situation
- Focusing on fixing problems instead of lamenting what's wrong
- Expressing our discontent in a healthy manner and then moving on

Positive Action Three: Live with a Smile

Smiling can affect how you live your life. Your language can affect what you believe. When you begin to change your physical actions and words to reflect a positive state of mind, your mind will often follow. When you decide that you will only say positive things, that you will laugh easily and often and that you will walk with a spring in your step, even if you have a headache, you are telling yourself that you are a positive person.

If you choose to live like a positive individual, you will become one. It's far easier to live a life of happiness and joy when you act like you are joyful. Walking around with a frown on your face and lamenting how tough life can be will undermine any of your efforts to develop a positive mindset. Why? Because we act how we believe! If someone was walking around crying about how unhappy they were all the time, why wouldn't we believe that they were unhappy? The more we behave as if we have a trait or quality, the better the chance we have of actually developing that quality.

To live life with a smile you can:

- Praise others often and with vigor

- Listen to music that uplifts you
- Make a point to dress colorfully and take care of yourself
- Repeat kind phrases to yourself and ignore negative self-talk

Positive Action Four: Find Positive People

We are creatures of social structure and when we surround by people who embody qualities that we want. We often adapt to behave like them. This can be a powerful tool or it can be a detrimental tool, it depends on who you are surrounding yourself with.

Many times we can find that we are surrounded by toxic people who drag us down. They might be negative individuals too and seek to keep the people around them to live just as negatively as they do. They might see people try to grow and heal in the world and scoff at them.

They could potentially drag you down, rather than help you get out of the negative patterns that have hurt you so deeply. Oftentimes it's because these negative people are still living in their false beliefs that things don't get better and they let their pessimism get the best of them.

On the flipside, you can find there are amazing people in this world who will do everything they can to help lift you up. Those are the kinds of folks you want to be around and while it might take some work, you can find them. Once they know what you're trying to do, that you want to live positively, they'll be there to help you move on up. You can learn a lot through imitation, so if you have a role model of positive thinking, learn as much as you can from them.

Many times in order to be able to develop a healthier positive outlook on life, we have to make the hard decision to limit our exposure to toxic individuals. This might feel somewhat painful at first, especially if we are someone that they depend on. But removing yourself temporarily from those who drag you down can have a very freeing effect on your life. It might be tough to do but in the long run you'll be much happier and more productive if you choose to walk away from those who do nothing but pull you down into their own, negative worldviews.

Positive Action Five: Dream Big

Dreams have a great value to the life of a positive thinker because they give you something to look forward to. There is a natural optimism in dreams and it's impossible to have a dream and be pessimistic at the exact same time! By making a point to allow yourself to dream big and to pursue after your dreams, you are explicitly saying "hey, I'm going to think positive here and nothing is going to stop me!"

Let your dreams be a little wild or unrealistic, it doesn't matter. The negative thought pattern says that everything is impossible but the positive thought pattern knows that as long as you give it your all, it doesn't matter how successful you actually are. Build goals, dream big and try your best. Don't worry about failure because fear of failure is a negative idea! Instead of being preoccupied with what you can't do, try to only look at what you can do! Think in terms of what you'll achieve, not in terms of what you "need to do."

Making the conscious decision to live out each day as a positive thinker isn't the easiest but after a while you will find that those thoughts will eventually become automatic. This time, instead of having to deal with overwhelmingly negative self-talk, you will find a calm, cheerful and reasonable voice emerge. This voice will definitely make a much better partner for the rest of your life. And isn't that what life is all about? We were not meant to have lives full of frustration and misery, rather our purpose was meant for things far better than negativity!

Conclusion:

Learning to think positive with action is not about repeating stock phrases and trying to trick yourself into feeling good. As we've seen throughout this book, the process of learning to think positively involves a lot of energy, effort and work. It requires reflection, introspection, patience and a willingness to involve one's self in the act of evaluating your own beliefs.

We don't develop negative beliefs overnight and likewise we don't eliminate them in a day either. It takes time and patience in order to bring about healing of the mind but it can be done! All you really have to do in order to develop a positive state of mind and learn to think positive is just focus on what you can do every single day. Each time you make the conscious choice to ignore the inner critic, each time you don't indulge in a pointless catastrophic fantasy or each time you resist the urge to automatically respond to stress, you are building yourself up to become stronger.

With each passing day, as long as you focus on developing yourself, looking forward towards the future and accepting responsibility for your life, you will find that you are capable of doing great things. You can have a life of positivity, happiness and joy, but it's going to take hard work to get there. Never doubt what the human mind is capable of doing, however, and don't think for even a moment that it's impossible. Challenge your beliefs, fight through the negative patterns and you will find that in time, your mind will adjust, adapt and grow to be as positive as possible.

We hope that you have been able to grow and learn from this book. It's been a long road and even as you look at what is ahead of you, we hope that you find excitement instead of dread. The rest of your life is a very long time, but the good news is that you can take positive thinking with you on that journey. Smile big, laugh often and ignore what the inner critic has to say. Live a life of positive thinking and take actions that reflect it!

Other books available by Michael Sloan on Kindle, paperback and audio:

The Art of Thinking Big: How to Establish and Reach Your Goals, Be Successful and Achieve Anything You Want In Life

The Art of Public Speaking: How to Speak In Front of an Audience without Fear

The Art of Problem Solving 101: Improve Your Critical Thinking And Decision Making Skills And Learn How To Solve Problems Creatively

Made in the USA
Middletown, DE
30 November 2016